APoCALYPSE MIX

APOCALYPSE MIX

JANE SATTERFIELD

Autumn House Press
Pittsburgh

Autumn House Press receives state arts funding support through a grant from the Pennsylvania Council on the Arts, a state agency funded by the Commonwealth of Pennsylvania, and the National Endowment for the Arts, a federal agency.

Cover photograph: Tanja Softić, *Migrant Universe: Departure Landscape*, 2008, acrylic, pigment, chalk on paper mounted on panel, 60"x120"/ 152x304 cm. Used with permission of the artist.
Book & cover design: Joel W. Coggins

ISBN: 978-1-938769-17-7
Library of Congress Control Number: 2016955582

Contents

IV

V

APOCALYPSE MIX

_1_

You have to deal with it

Strummer, Jones, Simonon, Headon, "Hate and War"

These days everyone wants
    two acres gated with herbicide. Everyone wants
      to eat high on the food chain while—

      Alice Fulton, "The Permeable Past Tense Of Feel"

Radio Clash

You'd have to travel back in time to find
the sound booth where we spun vinyl, blasting
tunes through dorms and dining halls, wave-

lengths of mild rebellion that never filtered
out beyond the campus gates to reach
the urban streets. You'd have to hunker down

inside those hacked, graffittied walls to read playlists
logged in marbled composition books by DJs
swamped with student debt, suited up in army

surplus gear. And was I what I played? Bleached
bangs and teased-out hair, up sometimes as late
as dawn hammering out prose so minimalist

nothing was left in. I was late to poetry, philosophy
of art, late *to the market to realize my soul*, no time to
stick around and smoke through Hard Rock Power

Hour with the Disco Redux guys. What couldn't
punk do if not make things burn a little brighter,
beat back the images burned on our brainpans:

strafe of jets against the sky, foliate walls of flame,
families bunkered down, and radioactive water
waste drifting downstream. . . . Out of luck and out

of love, *brew for breakfast*, tying up the tattered
laces of granny boots, of combat boots, a lick
of drugstore clear nail polish to keep the ends

from unraveling. Never the same river twice
when you're stepping through time and its
spinning door where *London Calling* spools

through Whole Foods' tinny sound system
years beyond that windowed sound booth
with its wall of outmoded knobs and dials

and switches where you watched the stylus
drop and let the record spin and spin as the center
blurred to black. And here they come—idling

through the aisles where other mothers pause
and hum, husband with *coupons from packets of tea*,
daughter with neon ear buds dangling—and those

power chords striking again and again, a sound
like sun burning through fog, like the sheer belief
anyone might blossom beyond some epic fail.

An Ideal for Living

Ian Curtis (1956–1980)

Beneath the flicker of fluorescent lights, the auras
of perfumed tea, double-strollers block the aisles.
Looks like we'll linger here a bit beneath the gaze
of flower-garlanded mannequins. Dear lady
of the artfully wrinkled Bermudas, destroyed
matchstick jeans and ballet flats—why is it this season's
psychedelic orange makes me think of detainees in stress
positions? Suddenly the volume's up, and I hum along, "Love
Will Tear Us Apart." How is it I've arrived here, teen in tow,
dear dress to impress with the vintage field army
watch, the studded leather belt? And what of ruined,
epileptic Curtis, winner in the suicide sweeps, Curtis
who crooned against a throbbing
bass line's frontal assault? Curtis who didn't live
long enough to hear his single—all-time great alt rock
anthem—become mere background noise?
How come I still hear the song as I first did, *authentic*,
on cassette, the dark tape spooling through my battered
Walkman? Dear dressing room with the hidden cam,
dear *but-I-digress*, the joke seems less witty now
as, pressed for an answer, I tell my daughter what
"joy division" is: nihilism, word play, doublespeak
for concentration camp prostitution wing.
Not the work of meaning, but the making of meanings. Again. . . Love. . .
In the afterlife of that atmospheric baritone, my teacher's discount
buys me a black dress, my daughter a headband of shimmering silk.

Elegy with Trench Art and Asanas

The studio door swings shut and Emily instructs us
to begin in an *easy seated position*. Eyes closed, we begin

to *check in*, to *be mindful of each feeling that rises.* Time
to think of some *intention*, something as simple

as the *reason that brought you to your mat*—that, not the noise
rising up from Stoneleigh Lanes, the business at basement level—

thunderous, I think, though nothing next to the volley of
shellfire and mines going off in the front's busier sectors—

strange sound track stuck in my hearing long after
I left the museum's cool halls, since I walked the wood-

planked trench alleys of the Great War Exhibit. Overhead,
dangling on cables above us, the artifact highlights—Fokker,

Sopwith, and Albatross; a shiny Pfalz acquired as part of Allied
War reparations—great flying machines manned by pilots

in both strategic bombing and battlefield recon runs.
But I'm *here*, *now*, to take in and tune out the noise of summer

camp duckpin party cheers, the detritus that lingers
in modern memory from a war so literary, delousing

was known as *reading one's shirt.* . . . Trikonasana's next to
strengthen the core: your ribs drop into the body's

fuselage. A deeper bend into the archival absence of cordite,
the scent of rust that still rises, post-rainfall, from the soil

of stricken villages across the French countryside.
In almost any of the English market towns I visited as a child,

my grandfather said to take notice when we reached the town
center—each marked by a concrete cenotaph, memorial

to lost fathers, sons, uncles, brothers, and fiancés. You might
find a stray paper poppy lifted, then dropped by the wind.

Emily advises us to *find your edge*. Boredom was just one of
many unspeakably awful trench conditions—and the lull

between morning stand-to and evening assaults meant anyone
might be taken out by a sniper's precisely aimed bullet. The efficiency

of England's postal service meant letters arrived with stunning ferocity,
making home seem distant yet paradoxically near. In situ,

soldiers chalked rocky outcrops; carved rings, crosses, or
pendants using spent bullet casings. Lighters might be fashioned

from greatcoat buttons. In Tadasana, the yogi seeks strength
from the earth, each breath a means to recharge *so long as*

it's kept as an active position. The more elaborate work that's found
up for auction these days—a shell-casing vase with the image

of two wounded Tommies approaching Dover's white cliffs
with the word *Blighty* hammered out gently beneath—would have

been the handiwork of blacksmiths or engineers in rear areas,
valuable based on who signed it, when, and where. The lamp

my daughter noticed displayed in the *Believe It or Not* Odditorium,
(your "drop-by for *a dose of weird*")—was probably scrap,

surplus repurposed post-battle or ready-made by locals (one man's
meal ticket, another's battlefield souvenir). My illustrated history

tells me each war *is ironic because each one is worse than expected*, though
this does not explain why we sustain, every few years at a time,

a renewable fashion for military chic. Dad was what? Ten, maybe
twelve, playing ball, when he lost the ring his father brought home,

something carved from the wing of a downed Messerschmitt.
How did his old man get it and where? When pressed

for more info on souvenir swag, when asked to decipher the
code of badges or slogans on T-shirts from Gulf One squadrons

my father passed on to his sons, there's not one I remember.
My husband jokes that I'm either playing dumb or don't

want to recall. To face the fear that darkens each day,
I've been told I need to learn, really, to breathe.

This studio runs sessions guaranteed to get me *up off the ground.*
Slung in a hammock over a mat—that's one way

to target areas for maximum results. With an amazing
power to cleanse, this is something more than (though it

resembles) circus-based aerial art. Across generations, panic's
rarely made pretty—but what of those vases, hammered

from artillery shells, the designs almost totally obliterated
thanks to assiduous dusting? In Shavasana, we seek sensory

withdrawal, an entry into deeper meditative states. After,
we must rise again to collect our things, walk past

the salons and boutiques that line this block, walk back
into our separate worlds. Sometimes we stop in the bakery

to pick up a coffee, trying not to flinch at the giant screen TV
with its flashing, disastrous crawl.

Triptych

I had a day's Underground pass, forms
to be filed for your passport. Soon,
we'd fly back to the States
if your paperwork was in order.
Your father stood watch in the embassy, ready
to call us in when needed, while I wheeled
you 'round the garden in summer's
equatorial heat. I shifted the sunshade
over your face.
                        Down the path, a stranger neared,
shopping bags in her hand, head scarf
adorned with flowers, petals scattering,
light and dark.

In this time before fear was everywhere,
what was the reason she caught my gaze?

§

Nearly two decades on, my screen flickers with images
of crowds and crusades, flags set aflame,
placards facing off outside the same American Embassy:
"Afghanistan's the graveyard of soldiers!", "If you want
Sharia, move to Saudi!" Rage tilts toward
extremes. Citizens are advised to review
the Worldwide Caution, stay current
with media coverage. The camera pans across
the roiling crowd, one side against the other: Londoners
who'd banish all immigrants, Muslim protesters
garbed in white.

How to speak
of what we share, what separates us?

If there's a woman in that crowd,
I don't see her,

§

                          but I remember the day
I waited with the pram, how you blinked
as I pulled back the sunshade and you tugged
your tiny bonnet, clenched fist unfurling.
In time's reflecting pool,
water gathers, builds to spill. . . That stranger,
alone, hesitant, reached in to touch your face—
What was her past? A dream of mosquito nets,
flashing rain? The cardamom pods
she'd bought for her mother?
                          She saw
a mum with a pram and neared, touching
the face of a stranger's baby, smiling
as she said *beautiful,*
as she said *blessed.*

Special Screening

Black Hawk Down, Towson Commons, Baltimore, January 2002

Tickets in hand, we take the escalator
to the second story of the Cineplex

where waiters cruise the crowd with
plates of chilled prosciutto, calamari, shrimp.

Olives, cheese, artisanal rosemary
bread. While wind shears the Commons'

wall, caprese stationed by the bar
seems slightly out of season. And though

some of us still stockpile Cipro, we toast
a season of good cheer, a New Year

where we are forward-looking. Just this week
the Senate Office Building's been fumigated

and reopened; doubled, the FBI anthrax
case reward. Here's a glass of good

Sangiovese, crowd patter, piped-in Eurovision
din, the line that forms where Bowden stands.

Who knows what war is like except
those who serve and those who care to ask,

take notes, tell the rest of us. . . . It's been
years since he's been in uniform, no fan

of nightly news, but Dad still wants to shake
this journalist's hand. House lights flicker,

there's applause as Eversmann and Blackburn
take their front-row seats. Here are Blackhawk

helicopters flying low along the coast, my
father saying *nothing like it, riding with*

the fly door open, the world going by
at however many thousand feet. Here are

Rangers roping into a teeming market place,
unexpected fire from RPGs. Here's gunplay

in Dolby Digital, Dad noting discrepancies
I'll read of later, in uniform, weapons, gear. Here's

a window into war, a fast daylight raid
gone wrong. In weeks to come we'll learn

much more of *unknown unknowns,*
the fog ballet of blood and ambush streets.

The varied means (and the charge this film was one)
of manufacturing consent. For now the house

lights going up, the soldiers escorted out
amid applause. Word has it the wind that's

kicking up may be a clipper bringing heavy
snow. We brace ourselves against the coming

storm, the fate of those who fight, those trained
to make a difference.

On Not Buying Vintage Oil T-Shirts at Old Navy

I

In the absence of severe alerts, we drove through the clearing
streets, past yards strewn

with storm debris, here and there dodging
a downed power line

to see where we might save a few cents at the pump.
We might well consider

this week's body count, the sorrow sustained in our announcer's
stern voice or the one tune

from the man at the top: *we must find alternatives to fossil fuel,*
same static we've been hearing

as long as we've been listening.

II

While shopping I was drawn to the discount table of vintage-style
tees, coveting the muted colors,

and old fashioned oil company logos, signposts of stations—
Texaco, Gulf, Esso, Sinclair—

seen from the back seat of Buicks, Grand Torinos, those gas-guzzling
family cars where we bounced along,

sans seat belts, watching the world go by. Today a corps of
engineers struggles with a containment

cap. With the right app, I could click as I shop, access
the list of federal

agencies involved in response to the gallons hemorrhaged
by a dynamically positioned

semi-submersible rig. Noise cannons keep birds from landing
in contaminated areas.

Apocalypse and empire—. We might wade out into silence.
And if later I somehow ease

into sleep, will I wake as I did more than a decade ago,
from the dream of rigs

burning a smoke script across the whirling desert sky?

Salt

Not apocrypha, as in Scipio salting
the Carthaginian fields, a curse
on reinhabitation; not the blacklisted
feature nor Jagger's salute

to the working man, but that
which purifies, preserves, seals
a bargain, signifies wisdom, intelligence,
and virility—. Or secrets

salted away, as in the ambition
a friend says she quickly learned
to kiss good-bye given that whole days
pass in the absence of any civil

workplace exchange. Work
that's meaningful, the new wisdom goes,
is work that's done with the hands. And here
I know I'll just have to defer, cross-cut

to conversations I overheard,
how they talked and sipped—mother,
aunt and uncle, looking back from
their vantage point on my backyard deck

to the hometown an ocean away,
looking back to the gilt light of *after the war*,
of *before the closure*
where mates from the mill are afforded

a moment to take a break from the line.
Salt of the earth, give you the shirt
off their back, everyone someone
you knew to nod to. And if those

smiles stay stuck in the space
of a frame tacked over my desk
almost half a century after the photo's taking,
am I to believe it's nothing more

than a publicity pose? Who's to say
camaraderie doesn't come from double-shifts
under blackout conditions, that
forging steel tubes for the Allied

under-the-ocean petrol pipeline
might account for some lingering
civic pride? The photograph does not

necessarily say *what is no longer*, but only
and for certain *what has been*. It *reminds us*
of its mythic heritage: group view
of the busted back, close-up of singed

coveralls—these are trims from the story.
With a simple click I can access the media
archive—*exterior shot of the town*
on a wet day, interview with the Labor MP

speaking on behalf of government agencies,
which cuts to *a view of workers*
who talk about the social consequences
of closure. And here, in this late luxury,

I'll try to construct my own *sottonarrativa,*
a smaller current in the larger river; I'll step out
of the shower, humming a little
"La Vie en rose" or the Kinks' "Get Back in Line."

There's no union man in sight
as I wander the aisles, considering
the virtues of each—coarse, finishing, flake,

gray, grinder, sea, smoked, or Sicilian—in
search of the imported butter that makes
my shortbread especially toothsome,
and caramels Fleur de sel.

Et in Arcadia Ego

After Sue Johnson's collage Edge of Town

If you're exhausted feigning interest
in sustainability initiatives, let me
be the first to extend an invitation
to the Utopia Motel, the paradise

that you were promised. Here where rubber
meets the road, we're bringing back
big cars, the relics of a better time.
You'll learn again that loving language—

exquisite fender, fin. I am in Arcadia also,
entrepreneur of extra butter fat. I mix
a mean grasshopper, surprise with
the pâté mold. I understand your deepest

need to live up to the part, to meet
all off-road expectations. That's why
there's parking here and plenty of it, door-
to-door, all the space the heart desires

for your much maligned SUV. No need
to clog yourself *with praises of*
the pastoral life. Clouds, you see,
are scarce or seeded here. Why

should sudden showers take you
by surprise, a storm disrupt
all that good motoring mojo? A perfect
picnic comes complete with cooling spray

delivered by a well-timed breeze or the dam's
daily flow variation. No mere mascot
for good living, I agree that *extraordinary*
places need not remain the property of the

elite. Forget Food Network and all those
fussy obligations, here's a dinner
tray, a view. What's good for
business is good for you—*the grass*

turns green unbidden. Feel free to
frolic on the median strip. We accept
all manner of assignations
and guarantee good sleep.

Malediction

Either you go
down this path
or you don't—

strewn with poison's
unholy trinity,
ivy, sumac & oak

that threads
summer's height:
a line of license,

of lit invitation,
the foxglove—bright
or moon-pale—

ringing its bells'
spotted throats.
Where wands of

wisteria whip wishes
that the cursed become
as liquid as water,

you go or you don't.
Stylus hammered
on scrap metal,

curse assembled ad hoc;
anathema, plague—
you go or you don't.

Where the yew
twitches missives
that *life & mind & memory,*

liver & lungs & words
& thoughts & memory
be mixed up together—

you go or you don't.
So consider, darling,
carnivorous love,

thirteen ways to look hot
while you're sweating.
Forgot something? Don't

worry; we thought so.
Here's sunshine beyond
bad luck's shadowed

reach, the lawn
where rabbits nibble
the new grass down to

its tenderest heart.

II

How promptly and ably
you execute Nature's policies
and are never

lured into misconduct
except by some unlucky
chance imprinting.

W.H. Auden, "Address to the Beasts"

Bestiary for a Centenary

*Animals were used in World War I on a scale never before seen—
and never again repeated.*

Alan Taylor, "World War I in Photos: Animals at War"

1

No one recruited them with posters
of trips abroad, obligations to protect
honor, or the "golden opportunity"
to "earn as you learn"—but
they also served in convoys &
calvalry, in pigeon schools & camel
corps; on land, in sky & sea, as
beasts of burden, scouts & spies,
mascots & more.

2

Tales abound
of boon companions—
pack-mule #141's
unbudging stance midway
across a footbridge
signaled where a five-
nine shell lay ahead.
At signal corps' command,
dispatch dogs with harnessed
spools of wire crossed ground
socked by autumn storms
& mortars' unspeakable
rain, dodging craters
deep enough to swallow
men to laying lines for
point-to-point field telephones.

Others shouldered baskets
of carrier pigeons into
forward lines. Terriers,
shepherds & bloodhounds
trained to search for wounded,
kitted out with Red Cross
gear in pouches on their backs,
heeled up with handlers
for inspection. Gas-masked,
outrunning sniper bullets, dogs
barreled through the lethal
fog of gas, that *Yellow Cross*

laid down by low-velocity shells
Doughboys & Tommies knew
as *Whizz-Bangs*, relaying
news through code notes
tucked in collars.

3

Some admirable combination
of compass sense & mapping
genius made carrier pigeons
ideal couriers for conveying
communiqués & maps
of enemy terrain. When field
telephone lines went dead
under heavy fire, their homing
skills could be counted on

to get a message through.
Set free from baskets & carrier
boxes in the trenches, they
raised alarms from scuppered
ships, or planes droning
on a death spiral, zeroing
back to where they'd first
been set to roost, guided
by signature designs painted
on the roofs of mobile lofts parked
behind busier battle sectors.

4

Of thousands employed
as urgent dispatchers in the age
before two-way radio broadcast
made mission tracking possible,
countless pigeons were intercepted,
shot, or shipped abroad, captives
paraded in home front streets.
Some were singled out for valor
& given medals with highest
honors. The last chance of a battalion
cut off in the Argonne, Cher Ami
flew through heavy fire, arriving
at his loft with a bullet in his breast,
message capsule dangling from
an injured leg. Today he stands
on one good leg, attentive as if
alive, poised in place among
entrenching tools, stick grenades,
prosthetic arms—museum memorabilia.

5

After battle rained down
grenades & gas in rounds
Yanks dubbed *Evening Hate* &
Enemy's Delight, one soldier's pet pit
bull, a stray smuggled from a shipyard
in the States, learned to track
no-man's-land for wounded men,
guiding the lost & disoriented
back to safety behind the line.
One day his bark alerted his unit:
an interloper sat trench side,
sketching, mapping out
the whereabouts of gunners,
ammo & supplies. Given rank,
"Sergeant" Stubby survived
seventeen battles & shrapnel
in his chest & leg, living on
to boost the morale of men
lodged in Red Cross recovery.

6

The litany of what newfangled
combat wrought for horses
is a history itself; their cries
at night etched the air.

One veteran recalled that sound
troubled him more than cries
from fellow men: *Because we knew—well
we presumably knew—what we were there for,
but them poor devils didn't, did they? No,
scores and scores of 'em* fell to barbed wire,
to bullets in the brain & worse
when mounts turned meals
for dogs & men. What to make of war's
strange economy: deep in combat zones,
glow worms, gathered in jars, gave off
reading light; even rafter rats crawled down
for crumbs of cheese, befriending
men in farmhouse billets *lying doggo*
before *zero hour* & Imperial sergeants
quipped that *silly blighters came for
free while horses cost good money?*

7

A hundred years: in farmlands,
forests & cratered ground, munitions
& the bones of missing men
keep turning up; honorary mayors
serve the memory of villages wiped
off the map. We have no name
for the scale of pain. A photo
shows the redolent sadness
of a draft horse hitched to post
moments after its partner perished
from a round of shrapnel; podcasts
bring other accounts to life—standing,
waiting, a shield, a spot of shade
against desert sun, these & others
also served: comrades & battle kin.

You went out to war.
War came over our house.

Muriel Rukeyser, "Welcome from War"

Our land is ploughed by tanks and feet

PJ Harvey, "The Glorious Land"

Parachute Wedding Dress

More fetching than the gowns
themselves, sail-white
and confectionary sweet,
are the stories concealed in
pieced panels, in cascades
of hand-edged, ruffled rows—

the work of savvy tailors
or sentimental brides
whose husbands-to-be
held fast to nylon or
best silk that saved them
as they sunk from sky to

beachhead, from burning
bombers to uncertain
fate in freezing fields
behind enemy lines. For his
fiancée's dream of a white
wedding dress, one survivor

in a displaced persons' camp
traded two pounds of coffee beans
and several packs of cigarettes
for a German pilot's useless
parachute. And on the close—
my mother's blacked-out English

street—canny mothers shared
out salvaged fabric for

hair ribbons and christening
gowns. How distant, now,
that world of rationed goods.

In museum cases, in picture-
perfect resolution,
such economy and love
handed on and handed down,
its life and afterlife.

On Listening to Elizabeth II's Secret WWIII Speech

Under the "30-year rule," the British National Archives releases confidential files to the public. Elizabeth's speech was read by an actor on BBC News UK Politics *on the web.*

When I listen online to a doomsday speech revealed
thirty years on from a Cold War scenario,

there's not a whiff of the archive's musty air.
But what broods here in late summer's heat?

In a live stream across the Atlantic, an actor delivers
words not from the Queen's own hand,

the script for a monarch schooled in disaster,
yet the speech still seems canonical in its call

to family & duty, to memory & shared inheritance—
the same mix of sorrow & pride recalled from nursery days

where, waiting by the wireless one September day,
a princess not yet a teen heard her father announce

war's onset. Within three years she'd record her first
speech, a broadcast to the Commonwealth's children,

those living with gracious hosts far from their homes
& those nearer, who'd weather the Blitz, *full of cheerfulness*

& courage, trying to do all we can to help our gallant sailors,
soldiers & airmen. . . trying, too, to bear our own share

of the danger and sadness of war. Still years from the crown,
she was already thinking of peace as work that falls

to the young.
But flash forward to the weeks,

storied & between seasons, where the warmth
of hearth & home, Yuletide & good cheer,

might have given way. The panic of air raids & conscripted
soldiers, the population in panic, as long-range

missiles approach, as embassies pool their shuttered
dark in the face of what's mad and MAD—

cities in ruin, topographies scraped off the map
in the broadcast that never took place.

Epistle with Invitation, circa 1916

For János Csillag, and others, called back to defend the Fatherland in the Great War

A blast from the past,
a way to get in the game,
which is to say that it arrived,
by telegram or post, in one
or more of the six languages
my father's Hungarian
grandfather spoke—citizen,
not scholar, of the shifting borders
a century mapped. Into what
stunned silence must this missive
have arrived, appeal & invitation
to come back & fight for
the Fatherland he'd abandoned
for steerage & a small farm
in West Virginia coal country. . . .
In the one photo I own, János' face
wears my father's, not stern
precisely, more like alert, piercing
eyes, the look of a man never glad
to suffer fools. Into what pile
of trash did he pitch the letter
into the midden of history, or into
what old-school, long-stem bent pipe
did he stuff it, lit refusals standing in
for thousands whose curses flew in Magyar,
Deutsch & more, *absolutely not,*
most certainly not, under no circumstances,
by no means, negative, never & nope,
uh-uh, nah, not on your life, no way
& ixnay & nem kell & nay inscribing the air
with a liberating beacon of smoke.

In Which She Considers Joining the Force

Morning's cake & rain & cups of coffee.
I can't see the mountain majestic
but there's a clearing called *where I might
have ended up*. There's 17 & who
I should date (or screw) & why (or why not);
what paths I should pursue, what future dreams
& fields of study—the list goes on & on. There's
the kitchen where coffee's brewing & the radio
shifts between stations, Dad's fatigues sudsy
in the daily wash. He's not alone in saying
that of all the ways to pay for college, this
might not be a bad one, when the Commander-in-Chief
holds in reserve one hundred Academy slots
for offspring of military men & women, retired
or serving in good standing. A bookish girl could do worse
than toughen up, study English & outwit Sallie
Mae. But I can't see myself as G.I. Jane, decked out
in olive drab. And though it's years until the Wall's
fall shreds the Iron Curtain, I fear a future
caught in someone's crosshairs, sandbagged
in a squadron like some frat house with guns.
Basic training might be worse: whose hands
might hold me down, a new recruit, my body for
the taking. . . . But my father only wants to help.
Some years are all unasked-for advice.
For now I'll fold the sergeant's standard issue
tees, pour the coffee, take another sip.

Souvenir

Friendly fire, parasites &
tropical disease, depleted
uranium lodged
under the skin, exposure
to pesticide, mustard gas,
Sarin, combat stress, muscle
twitching, memory loss
& the whole host
of "mysterious symptoms"
experienced by troops
located downwind
from burning oil wells
& chemical weapons
demolition depots—
& although my father evaded
these dangers simply
because he was deployed—
quartermaster & answer man—
with a tactical airlift
refueling wing, as far
as he can figure,
the persistent ear trouble
goes back to his days
in the desert. Who'd
need an official report
when common sense suggests
the causes of hearing loss
are as simple as noisy
engine rooms & aircraft
uptake & of course sand
& dust & whatever drifted

into the synthetic cells
of protective plugs & Mickey
Mouse ears & if it's his
fate to deal with systematic
antifungal treatment for
an itch that's untreatable, *so
it goes, never a bad that
couldn't be worse.* Distant
as the whir of choppers,
the *what what what* my father
no longer asks, having learned
to turn his one good ear
toward or away as the
conversation suits. No doubt
you recall the ticker tape
parades, free passes for
amusement parks, cruises,
hotels & other deep discounts
by which we could show
sufficient thanks, seal our
belief in fair compensation.
Headsong & *humsickness*
are a few of the names
given to earworms,
those sticky tunes you
can't get out of your head,
the product of some memory-
based cortical itch. With
luck you can locate
a good eraser tune to shift
the stubborn soundtrack.

Field Manual for the Forgotten

May 21, 2011, the date predicted for "the Rapture"
by evangelical Christian radio host Harold Camping

After we've played our Apocalypse
Mix, after late lunch and presents and just

as the sun starts to slip past the mid-
afternoon mark on the late May day that's

my daughter's sweet sixteenth, just when she's
left at the hour appointed by law to ensure

she divides her time equally between parental
homes, no sooner than I've started

to pour something chilled, my father—
who's said not very much all day, who's

thrown no more than his share of jokes into
the mix—suddenly decides it's his turn

to talk. Any hope of a festive anecdote's
blown when the story's a monsignor's

funeral down county, meaning a round of
local news I've missed—that, and the vats

of hundred-degree bitter coffee, foiled chocolates,
sugar cookies, cheese platters, the bottomless

bowls of pink or green freezer punch for mourners. . . .
And maybe I'm wifty after a little wine, or just

zoning out in the heat, so maybe I miss
some crucial detail of my brother's classmate's

sudden and apparently inexplicable death;
how he woke one day to a black blotch on his shin

and died within a few weeks. It's years since I thought
of the "Tower of Doom," a Cold War relic

at the former biowarfare center in Frederick,
the (surely) tall tales we kids told about the Anthrax

Building, the research labs, and just how much
I hated to set foot on that base.

What we took for fact: that in the seven-story
all-but-windowless building lurked three-story

tanks for bio-agent production, catwalks where
workers on high floors could watch those below,

thick-gloved, white-coated wizards bent to their work,
"kill" tanks nearby to render chemicals harmless.

The doors, we heard, worked on some elaborate
ventilation system to keep contaminants

under containment. And on the long-ago day
of some rumored spill, a bloom of bubbling toxic

flora, the building was evacuated, blockaded,
then sealed. Not yet forty, my brother's friend,

an active reservist, this father of three, whose mysterious
symptoms, were, in the end, never explained.

No refill, thanks, for my father, who's not much for
close questioning—who, even though he's retired,

still sticks to the scripts of his youth: NSA equals
No Such Agency. Time for me to cue a few clouds, bring

out what's left of the cake. I'll get nothing more from him beyond
a shrug, or a half-muttered phrase, *Poor kid, some unspecified work.*

Combat-Ready Balm

No contest at $12.50 a jar—a must-have for the medicine
cabinet, soothing salve for sand-flea bites,

sunburn and dry skin, a cocktail of good wishes
wrapped in field green and red trim, hopeful

appeasement like the St. Christopher medal I gave my dad
after the 459th's midnight call, the usual round

of inoculations, the botulinum and anthrax vaccines.
Just like that, he was part of the mission,

off to Gulf One with the Military Airlift Command, nothing
like flying the friendly skies. Just like me to offer

an apocryphal saint as protection, a saint whose feast day
was dropped from Church record in the absence of any

historical evidence he'd ever existed. You've heard
those stories of letters, notebooks and Bibles tucked

into breast pockets, how they could stop a bullet's path?
There's no shame in sending loved ones off with a charm.

Patron of travelers, invoked against storms and plagues and every
etc., does it matter if Christopher's simply a stand-in

for the soul treading turbulent waters? About the balm itself, well,
it's good to know it's environmentally friendly, essential

oils, no petroleum, nothing synthetic—especially good
given the billions it costs to outfit tents with AC,

good given the dangers to troops on the ground who move fuel
to distant outposts via a network of slightly up-graded

goat trails. I hate to think of the youths
and family men and women lining up at Air Mobility

Command, the same site where they filmed the video promotion
for Combat-Ready Balm's Operation Sand Flea.

Once, I boarded an Air Canada flight, a soldier smiled,
looked straight into the camera, saying nothing

of stress or mission fatigue. Smiling, in desert camos,
commissioned to say how much he wants us to know

how even a small thing helps. Nearly twenty years on,
uniform turned in, my father's still wearing his medal.

Object Lessons

Autodidacts of semaphore & Morse,
we ranged through ragged suburban

lots & basements lit by screen loops
of combat scenes on land, in sky & sea—

the same screens simulcasting hijinks of draftee
doctors gathered around a still somewhere

in Korea, jerry-rigged from junked parts,
bubbling on before the drone

of choppers brought in one more wave
of wounded. . . . We were also-rans

at War's long slap-hand campaigns,
those card battles carried on porch-side, pool-side,

sheer relief while the Watergate hearings rumbled
on. O board games where we learned strategems

of risk & subterfuge, bluffing & bomb
placement, misdirection, the proper

use of scouts & spies. . . . One takeaway
from my grandmother's government-sponsored

travel club tour behind the Iron Curtain
was hurled fast at our shows of

impatience: faced with the endless line
at a single ice-cream kiosk, everyone—

she swore—was happy with whatever flavor
was handed over. In today's lull

between parades & fireworks,
I'm leaning into streets so empty

I catch the quality &
pitch of birdsong, the hum

of laundry snapping on lines—all
of which would—in disaster—

flame & fuse. Summer & winter
we prayed for the conversion of Russia, greedy

hands grabbing Atomic Fireballs, bomb-
pops frosted red, white & blue.

IV

An immigrant to the United States from Bosnia, once part of Yugoslavia, I am fascinated by questions of cultural identity or cultural belonging on an intellectual level but I experience and feel what Edward Said called "the contrapuntal reality [of an exile]" very acutely: I have transitioned through three citizenships in addition to one period of being a citizen of no country. In both my new and old countries, outdated notions of national and ethnic identity and belonging continue to shape the politics and the society.

The visual vocabulary of *Migrant Universe* drawings suggests a displaced existence: fragmented memories, adaptation, revival, and transformation. . . Remembering becomes an act of reconstruction, where one works with what is there and tries to visualize what has been lost.

Because each act of memorization necessarily involves interpretation, there can be no objective recollection. Nor is there full erasure; like matter, memory seems to persist by transforming.

Tanja Softić, artist's statement on **Migrant Universe***, her series of paintings*

MIGRANT UNIVERSE

Between two worlds
life hovers like a star.
Byron

The Map of What Happened

Searches, arrests, and attacks, injuries to bystanders—the specter of arbitrary detention, of road blockades. . . So the storyteller picks her way. . . .

The soul may well recoil at *the bomb-gutted station, the houses laid open to the elements still bearing within their rubble outlandish bits and pieces of what had once been security. . . .* Areas of interest, archipelagos of safety, and overhead—the rook or the raven. More than one makes *an unkindness, a murder* if you're speaking of crows.

Situational awareness might mean many things: adherence to mission, intelligence in enemy terrain, which weather, which troops, other support available. Do tram lines or thoughts account for these dense tracings, are they dendrites or air traffic patterns? Injurious and purifying—this flame.

Lost among them, all I needed was the name of a small ridge, a local custom, a cell of this historical animal—the map of the world, my sojourn, and other shadings of memory: *let them burn me clear of attachment.*

Angel of Absence

Note in passing that one landscape bleeds into the next: the midsummer field's soon shot over with a silhouette of your hometown square. Note in passing *some of the walls have been whitewashed...* Track shadows, echoes, scents; track prints and the grainy dust of blitz sites.

Unbidden, the angel of absence arrives. Unbidden, the angel of absence will drape these beads, these blessings, this dark bouquet. Will upend any notion of absolutes. Abides no citizen's outmoded coinage. Unbidden, the angel of absence extends a companionable arm. Insists you hold these countries close... ensures you walk aware of *other shifts of emphasis, erosions, contractions, and croppings.* After the forays have ended, the angel of absence lifts.

Years later, tickets and wishes, timetables, stamps, and identity cards tumble from a book's cracked spine.

On each other's hands who care... on the side of angels in pleasure parks, cul-de-sacs: the perfumes of distance and local cuisine and the fountain empty in the market square where once you stood seraphic.

Second Angel

Something's decided to narrate in more dimensions than I can know: this angel's transmission across time and space. Telegraph towers mapping the tangle of transit. *When I go back, I feel exiled from it all. . . And always there are two thoughts, one cutting through the first until it isn't there. . .*

The habitual dreams: the road away, the bombed-out station. Concerning the centrality of the spoken word, concerning arcane markings, thresholds, fences and bridges—.

Concerning the heat: heraldic in the depots of time. Through the scrim of leaves overhead, through the scrim of habitude, through the scrim of all we inhabit, these husks gathered at da   Rendezvous at messenger nine.

Or think how we hacked through woods to emerge at a temporary clearing— the storied dusk. The hum overhead.

In the here and now—the map packed and secure. Messengered to me.

Landscape and Departure

Diplomatic pouches, cryptic postcards—always *some kind of map stretching beyond these lines:* history, politics, progress. . . . Memories dimmed to the quality of ancient murals. . . . I find a new road I never knew existed or, is it an old street deprived of its landmarks?

Flight path of crows, drone of a crop duster, make a U-turn, stop at the light. A richer soil, a sunnier nook—magazines and morale builders. . . sheen of sleeping water in winding canals. . . *If there is rain or a guard. . . prepare to leave/seem to have just arrived.*

Sweet scarlet branches, forgotten species, first swallow of wine—so we name our constellations.

Evangelist

Who calls it forth—wash of forgotten song, itinerant flora, whorl of whelk, web of hand upheld in benediction? *A field like no other: heaven above it; heaven below....* And the evangelist—zealous silhouette, scribe.

These leaves, these empty serving bowls—signifying sustenance given, sustenance sought. *Message after message after message—who is sending them? Just who are they for? Poor soul reduced to just one string....*

Angel of Becoming

A rain of exile—abundant, viscous, dense—pouring from the high cubes of a city's cement....

The angel of becoming knows looking's not the least of our pleasures so when the sky goes dull and daylight fades there's escort, encounter, the atlas upended . . . dark branch overhanging, memory as messenger (mined)....

Think checklist, think star chart and compass rose.

Think all manner of caution: strong tide here, foul ground there.... His charge: *to revive this chilled portion of your life and restore it to warmth....*

In greenhouses and gardens the other landscapes became mine—the double gates, the lines of taxis, the accent of the tongue, the accent of the soul. Field scored, horizon shifted. The footpath like the view from the barn.

Fragments of Joplin, x's look of amusement. . . and on this road there are many signs. Riffs overheard, the ruins, the music. . . buried beneath new impressions, trampled between resurrected ones....

Experiment with a new stove in the kitchen, produce an unusual dish *the same magistrates, procurators, and councilors—sun, moon, and morning star, summer solstice, winter solstice, equinox. Arcturus and Draco, the seasons of sowing and planting* as an antidote to sentiment, as an open door.

The sound of wings, of riffling papers.... As the crow flies, as the crow calls— writing a letter, sealing it, writing the address then the stamp becoming un- stuck.

Revolution

The dead hand of history tells the beads of time. . . . Forcible and *overthrow; gruesome but necessary. . . .* Here at the storied crossroads *ordinary members of the public, hooligans, arsonists, rioters, serial killers. . .* borrowed costumes and battle cries: bunkers, barbed wire, the bronze heroes along the boulevard. . . .

When I left, there was no time to look back—demonstrations, disruptions, speeches, and ceremonies. . . the pigeon park, the shopping plazas, the shelling at close range.

If the old songs were onto something, need we say it was good? The beads of time tell. *Orbit, circular course* or try this: Late Latin, meaning *rollback, wide-reaching change.*

An anchor, a star map—wreaths and garlands as once more the rain relaxes its guard.

V

The anguish of the earth absolves our eyes
Till beauty shines in all that we can see.

Siegfried Sassoon, "Absolution"

The flowers bloom where you have placed them.

*Victor Krummenacher, Greg Lisher,
David Lowery, Chris Pedersen, "Sweethearts"*

For Virginia Woolf, March 28, 2011

House damp, house untidy. Winter's lyric mood. Who seeks a versatile vegetable for a chilly spring hears Tomahawks scream over someone else's skies. A bomb drops, a window rattles. From underneath, where you were watching, danger appeared: *a silver pencil, a plume of smoke*. Walks which had given delight, walks which had given words. Then the greatest pleasure in town life gone. Prayers and anthems—the thought of peace like a sawing of branches overhead. Like a desperate illness, punctual as vespers. Routed today by clearing out our kitchen. Sausage and haddock. One writes, gains a certain hold. Then the zoom of a hornet which—any moment—might sting you to death. Just a piece of studio wall standing. Otherwise, rubble where I wrote so many books. *As the foxhunter hunts, as the golfer golfs.* One pilot landed safe in a field. You can't think what a raging furnace—open air where we sat so many nights, gave so many parties. Searchlights, a sense of invasion. How close it comes—hum and saw and buzz all around us. Allies holding. The marsh soggy and patched with white. *To soldier on, even in the thick.* A stone, a walk, a little before noon. Two very small lambs staggering in the east wind. Shall I write. . . *something grieving and tender and heavy-laden and private?*

Elegy with Civil War Shadowbox

In the wake of the towers' collapse, there were emails and memos,
strategic advice for teaching about terror. After a day off for mourning,

with class back in session—from phone calls, floor meetings, and vigils—
students were simply tapped out. In time we'd send our support—

in the form of chocolate, baby wipes, and Skin So Soft—to desert troops.
But for now—collective dreams spattered with ash—comfort came

in simply turning back to our work, one way to counter catastrophe.
And in the days that followed, we wondered how to pay tribute to what

is simply beyond words. Clearly the question haunted John Philemon Smith,
teacher and town historian, eyewitness, at seventeen, to the battle

that *transformed his hometown from sleepy village to a mass grave.* Over the course
of the twenty-four years that followed, in treks along Antietam Creek,

across twelve miles of countryside, in sorties back into memory's terrain,
to phantom gunfire and visions of *riflemen kneeling on the bodies of the slain*

to fire at retreating survivors; into the ghost-cries of a Gaelic charge from the Irish
brigade, the pile-up of the wounded, and slow work of the Burial Crew,

he gathered whatever the ground gave up, assembling a shadowbox from battle
debris: a folding camp spoon, Union uniform buttons, fragments of spent

artillery shells, minié balls, a belt buckle, fragments of a bayonet. Across the back
and sides of the box, in Smith's upright and legible hand, details of battle, news

clippings, lines from an official's commemorative speech. Rhymed quatrains
citing *plenteous funeral tears, the neighing steed, the flashing blade,* trumpet blast and

cannonade; his hand-carved replica of the cemetery's Private Soldier Monument
placed front and center to create a compelling visual field—one man's memento

of hope and healing that left out conflicts still simmering—segregation's
mark in the veteran burials from the world wars. I remember the heat-stunned

and rutted dust of Bloody Lane, scant chirp of crickets, wind, a park ranger's
period details—shells exploding the pacifists' church where wounded

were taken, the shallow graves "common as cornstalks" in family fields.
The emancipated would wait more than a year for the state

to rewrite the law and grant them freedom. Later, while slathering ears
of Silver Queen with butter and salt, it was hard not to think

of troops taking cover in cornfields, restless in the hours before dawn.
Around our battered kitchen table, twenty-some miles from that field,

squabbles grown silent, my brothers with their biblical names,
spared the call of conscription, bowed their heads for grace.

Crossing the Shenandoah in Late Summer

I

I was the back-seat bore, the poor passenger
while our family station wagon rode the hairpin turn
that crossed from one state to the next—

Why do we have to move out to the sticks? I complained,
14 & restless, in running shorts & grass-stained Keds. The day
was deep in cicada hum, in the thrum of white-water

as the current rushed across shale plateaus
toward the confluence of rivers. Where traffic slowed near a roadside stand
sizzling with corn & BBQ, I caught sight of our thriving divisions:

parked on the shoulder, a Chevy pickup, its gun rack
draped in the Stars & Bars. I'd get used to seeing that banner.
A Klan Grand Dragon lived in the town that bordered

Jefferson, our new home. For years, protests overruled,
the hooded marchers' rallies were sanctioned as "free speech."
Nearby churches held prayer vigils. Locals hoped it would rain

"to beat hell." But fuzzy footage of white-robed citizens—"200
White gentile persons" gathered so people could "see our side"—
still hovers online, on screen.

II

The Internet blows up with news of the gunman, 21,
who shot 9 worshippers at Bible Study in the Charleston A.M.E.—
young killer whose jacket displayed the flags

of fallen Apartheid regimes & I discover
my own state flag bears emblems of secession. Regiments
opposed to the Union fled south under red-

&-white "Crossland colors." They fought for a life
that relied on men, women & children
shackled & transported. The panoramic view where

those rivers collide, Jefferson wrote, was *worth a voyage across
the Atlantic.* In the century that followed, the abolitionist
John Brown named *the crimes of this guilty land,* seized

arms to mount a slave rebellion & was sentenced
for treason. If we had stopped on that summer day
& I'd have dared to ask that driver why he flew the Confederate

flag, what would he have said in defense?
Pride & heritage, liberty? I'm still staring at that open secret.

Cursing for Beginners

'Curse tablets' are small sheets of lead, inscribed with messages from individuals seeking to make gods and spirits act on their behalf and influence the behaviour of others against their will. The motives are usually malign and their expression violent...

What options were available to the victims of theft or other crime?... For those lacking [political] connections, divine patrons, appropriately addressed, were perhaps the only hope.

Curse Tablets from Roman Britian (website)

Let the tablet of lead nix
nicety's danse macabre.
Let it wreak vengeance
for linen and luck stolen,
let it speak appeals gone
unheard, cases that get
no traction, injuries
at the hand of civil servants,
undutiful daughters, underlings
bearing bouquets of nettles green
as mint with the venom
of hidden sting. Let it stand
for the wish to dull and fatigue,
bring to account, exact and redeem
money or malice; with repeated
prayers and coin, make weary with
every hardship. Cross-hatched with runes
and the morning's epigraphs of light,
let it be folded and fixed, stabbed
seven times, needled with pins
and nails. Driven down
into a spring or sunken pool,
legible to the god alone, let this
memorandum guarantee no rest

before/unless/until. Who has acted badly,
been poorly disposed, or privy to this
taking away, whether slave or free, male
or female—in the absence of concord
or complete amends, let there be
no buying-off these provocations unless
with their own blood.

Resurrection Spell

. . . I could swear sometimes you're there,
Returned to me as wind—behind the nodding leaves.
    Sarah Hannah (1966–2007)

Good friends who wish for a resurrection
spell often employ elegy—from antiquity,
a song of mourning or lamentation. If I
conjure formal feeling, shards of ritual, kin,
forgive me, too keen to call the lost one
to cross over. To keen is to cry, weep, wail
at all that's beyond our ken. *Breath,*
blood, bone. The universe at odds
with our will. How *the hardest thing*
in this world is to live in it. If a spell
requires skillful practitioners, I'm sure
I'll come up short. For elegy spells
loss, a succession of lines penciled
over fine paper which must possess
exactly the right surface to support
details and precise tonal gradations—scatter
of laughter, a few blue skinks
across a stone wall or stalled there
in a blade of late afternoon light. Let's draw
a protective circle at night, put
on the kettle to brew. Who's to say if,
at any moment, you might breeze back
into the studio kitchen. Half-shriek,
half-song, outlawed and outmoded,
in eyewitness accounts the keen
lives on, a choral practice that came
to accommodate all manner
of praise and social critique. From antiquity,

these stagey ways to garb
our grief. Spell me with something
auspicious, a glass of said ale, Abbey style,
with its five types of barley malt, and the
dormant hops the brewmaster brought back.
To life and afterlife. Bottle
or can, flavorful and not too sweet.

Last Dinner at Louie's with Levis

Louie's Bookstore Café, Baltimore, 1992

Not the chichi place that supplanted it—gold sheers
and archaic columns—but the arty bookstore café
some short steps from monument and museum.

Café of ambition, ambivalence, indolence,
of all nighters, mornings after, café where I bought
Bernhard and Borowski, Heaney and Herbert,

café of gravy-slopped fries by the platter
to share, café of blinking, low-wattage bulbs
whose smoke-reek brought on grievous migraines,

café where I chugged espresso to hear—for once—
the heart resound in my chest, café where Levis
is talking to us, twenty-somethings wreathed

in the afterglow of simply being invited along.
There's the perfectly poised conversational tone
in which he described the "three-dollar vision"

of a mescaline trip, the high church hush
as we took it all in, leaning a little closer above
the clink of glasses, the stereo's rising volume—

There's Levis, *a rule breaker, someone important*—
There's how he stirred coffee, simply, with no sign of flourish,
didn't once betray any boredom—if he even felt it—

going through one more gig. There's the tattered
sleeves of my cardigan edged with ink, as if I'd authored
a book called *Earnest.* What a phrase like "the look of distance"

might mean to the one teller of the tale, talking
to a table of listeners who'd climbed rickety stairs
to a corner table as if it were an understanding

at which they'd arrived—. There are field notes
for the vision quest I never had, how these days
my hunger's for quiet, mostly, and a little peace. . . .

There's the way anything said in passing
can grow so much larger than life, how by the time
dessert arrived with its garnish of white and dark chocolate curls,

the conversation took on the patinated finish of anything lost
to time. There's how elegy is not commodity,
not a comestible, even though it inscribes a long-gone

invitation to *pick up a fork and dig in.* There's how
I could walk up the block to that refurbished storefront,
where breaking and entering's the only means of admission,

a tactic, which seems like a desecration of memory
which assumes its own style and means
of embellishment. Memory which is nothing

if not aspirational, no matter the affectations
it's picked up, throwing locutions like *truly diabolical food*
into the mix. There's the fist raised, about to smash

that plated glass storefront window and the way something else

will always intrude like the authentic rattle of boxcars
into the night, freight thrumming through a Virginia field,
which already starts to sound like lament,

a full moon glazing summer's already wizened grass.

Affinity with Orwell

In those days an enthusiasm for the adverse,
no one knew the depth of what had been done,
un-authoring letters, adjusting lists
as I took my turn at tables tossing back
ever-lusterless hair. *My carte d'identité*
was not enough—two shabby overcoats,
a cardboard case. My sister spoke only of *E*,
the front man's hand-rolled cigarettes, walks
in the woods waiting for words, another intoxicant
to take its effect. Nights I spent on my script, lured
on by the promise of an island address. . . . That's
what I called style—where I woke—*no more*
than the fringes: pastures drenched with rain,
lungs filling with second-hand smoke.

In a Time of Troubles

Europa Universalis invites players to explore wartime scenarios through various eras and cultures, from Ancient Rome to the Napoleonic Wars.

Noxious heat descends, the possibility
of plague & an event chain
that includes revolt risk

& stability cost. Avoid the hazards
of sitting all day. Even in games
of grand strategy, ruler

popularity suffers from plain old
public fatigue. Asked for their expertise,
old gamers scroll through calamities

like beads on a chain—drained coffers,
diplomatic points spent, failure in missions
undertaken on a nation's account—

chronic catastrophes to be solved
with manpower replenishment.
No need to abstract

out women characters—in Roman Britain
they can function as warriors, take full
lead in the field. Trade nodes

increase bonus points, so try acquisition,
annexation, leaking trade to
pirate nations, though this, too

might spark another revolt.
There's bound to be a huge
barbarian uprising when

least expected. Don't worry
about a first go-round demise:
no one conquers the world

on the first try. Site crashes won't pose
much of a problem. With patches
& expansions, it's easy to reassign provinces,

countries & cultures. It's easy to play
as Carthage & win. The optimism idea
keeps up an army's rating, but an empire

doesn't have infinite will. Be warned
that the vision may not be backward
compatible. Better to sign a peace treaty

than slog through a long campaign.
Concentrate armies to avoid
attrition. Because it wasn't bad enough once,

you can rewrite history, undertake
another installment of domination,
create unique stories of conquest.

You have the conquistador helmet. Click sieges,
characters, armies, authority.
Click epic & definitive list.

Why I Don't Write Nature Poems

Because I'm always wearing the wrong shoes, I rarely stray from the path. There's *recollect*, there's *tranquility* and the way the trains punctuate each hour, shrill the shaken fields. Let's bide a bit here, thinking why we love them—the tracks, the transit, *a train's a metaphor for so many things in life*. Like me, too busy eyeing up the buffet from the back of the line to consider a phalanx of phlox, the tabby stray cavorting in the hedge. I don't see a cow meadow as any kind of invocation. Am drawn to the satellite dish disrupting the view. To the one swatch of sky where the haze hangs. Because, truly, the one time I tried, the saddled mare extended an answer. The hoof on my foot a fine form. Because the genius of the place can drop a scroll of sycamore bark at my feet, and I still can't translate his tongue. Slow study. What happens in the ditch, the dun. Because a cicada's buzz in the topmost branch is all the intel left to get, trilling, a telling: *here, here, I am here.*

Portuguese Man o' War

Full sail, a feat
of stylized rigging,
armed frigate, eating machine
whose armadas blow ashore
through warming currents,
to cooler coasts off Amagansett,
up the Atlantic as far north as the Bay of Fundy,
The Isle of Man—and I
who envisioned your technicolor
rays only in *Our Amazing World's*
slick pages, centerpiece of
danger and display—how you swim
up unbidden, struck chord
like the wail of sirens, the *warning*
and the *all-clear*, the stark list
of grocery stash guaranteeing
post-atomic household survival. So you drop
that fine-spun glass pane
at the first sign of surface threat
to submerge or travel dark, lucent pools—
O blue bottle, spilled ink—
Even dead you deliver a sting.

Notes

Elegy with Trench Art and Asanas: Italics in lines 19 and 39 are drawn from Sterling's 2009 illustrated version of Paul Fussell's classic critical study, *The Great War and Modern Memory.*

Triptych: Inspired in part by Bhanu Kapil Rider's *The Vertical Interrogation of Strangers.* I filed a request for citizenship for birth abroad of an American citizen on my daughter's behalf at the American Embassy in 1995. At the same site, during the moment of silence on 9/11/11, protestors set a flag on fire.

Special Screening: Following the 9/11 attacks, a number of public officials and US Senators received letters laced with anthrax sent via the US Postal Service. Cipro, an oral antibiotic given to those exposed to anthrax, was distributed to high-level government officials and widely sought-after by a portion of the citizenry. Soldiers in attendance at the Baltimore screening were SSG Matt Eversmann (leader of the US Army Rangers Delta Force Blackhawk helicopter crew downed in Mogadishu) and crewmember PFC Todd Blackburn.

Salt: Describes footage recorded in 1979 by *Midlands News* as steel workers and townspeople in Corby, England faced the imminent closure of Stewarts and Lloyds Steel Works. During WWII, the mill contributed to the Pipe-Lines Under the Ocean Operation, producing steel pipes to transport fuel for the D-Day invasions. Italics in lines 40-42 are drawn from Roland Barthes' *Camera Lucida.* Charles Wright's concept of sottonarrativa appears in lines 52–53.

Et in Arcadia Ego: Italicized phrases are excerpted from work by Frank O'Hara, Theodore Roosevelt, and Virgil.

Malediction: Italicized phrases are excerpts of inscriptions from a curse tablet discovered in a thermal spring in Bath, England.

Bestiary for a Centenary: Useful sources included: Alan Taylor's ten-part series "World War I in Photos," which appeared online at *The Atlantic*; the Imperial War Museum's "Voices of the First World War" recordings; Richard Ben Cramer's "They Were Heroes Too" (*Parade Magazine*); Jasper Copping's "Honoured: the WWI pigeons who earned their wings" (*The Daily Telegraph*); Mike Dash's "Closing the Pigeon Gap"(*Smithsonian Magazine*); and *Time*'s "Top Ten Heroic Animals."

In Which She Considers Joining the Force: Helen Benedict's incisive writing about women in the military offered insight and inspiration.

On Listening to Elizabeth II's Secret WWIII Speech: MAD—or mutual assured destruction—was an essential doctrine of Cold War military strategy. Once the USSR had achieved nuclear capabilities equivalent to the US, both countries faced complete annihilation in the event of either side's strike. Princess Elizabeth's 1940 broadcast is available in full on the BBC archives.

Field Manual for the Forgotten: Building 470, a seven-story brick-tower laboratory located on the Fort Detrick Army base in Frederick, Maryland, was the site of biological warfare research production from 1954 until it was blockaded and sealed in 1969. The facility continues as a base for biological defense research.

Migrant Universe: Tanja Softić's *Migrant Universe* paintings together form a lyrical meditation on exile, memory, and longing. The sequence here incorporates a chorus of voices, among them: Kay Boyle; Michael Ondaatje; Breyten Breytenbach; Ciarán Carson; John Berryman; Roy Fisher; Larry Levis; Aleš Debeljak; Vasko Popa; John Matthias and Vladeta Vuckovic (co-translators of the Serbian epic poem, *The Battle of Kosovo*); Ivo Andrić; Albert Camus;

Plutarch; Ruth Prawer Jhabvala; Glenway Wescott; Homi Bhabha; Anders Behring Breivik, and Hans Magnus Enzensberger. More information on the artist's work is available at tanjasoftic.com.

For Virginia Woolf, March 28, 2011: Woolf died on March 28, 1941. The poem is a mashup of several sources: these include Woolf's entries from *A Writer's Diary* as well as her 1940 essay, "Thoughts on Peace in an Air Raid."

Elegy with Civil War Shadowbox: The Antietam National Cemetery Memorial Shadowbox, ca. 1886, created by Smith, is part of the Maryland Historical Society's American Civil War collection. Line 29 includes a quotation from a letter written by Samuel Michaels, son of a Sharpsburg farmer.

Crossing the Shenandoah in Late Summer: Harper's Ferry, West Virginia marks the convergence of the Shenandoah and Potomac Rivers; Jefferson's observations of his visit to the area are included in *Notes on the State of Virginia* (1785). The Maryland State flag is comprised of two heraldic crests from the coat of arms of colonial proprietors, the Calvert family. Prior to the Civil War, the state banner displayed the yellow-and-gold bars known as "Baltimore" or "Maryland" colors; afterward, the red-and-white or "Crossland colors" were incorporated to inspire post-war unity. Useful sources included Chip Brown's "Klan's Planned Rally Jars Tranquil Life of Md. Community" (*Washington Post*, June 27, 1980) and photographs of Frederick, Maryland at Getty Images.

Cursing for Beginners: "In theory in Britain Roman law applied to Roman citizens and local laws to non-citizens... However in an 'under-policed' society, it was necessary to use social or political connections to bring the law to bear" (from the Curse Tablets from Roman Britain website). The tablets found at Roman archeological sites in England provide phrases included in several lines of this poem.

Resurrection Spell: Adapts language from the two-part "Bargaining" episode of Joss Whedon's *Buffy the Vampire Slayer.* Resurrection Ale is a popular Baltimore microbrew.

Last Dinner at Louie's with Levis: Line 15-16 paraphrases a line from Levis' poem "In 1967." Line 19 incorporates reflections from Levis' 1982 interview with David Wojahn which appears in *The Gazer Within*. Edward Byrne's essay "To Recover the Poet: Larry Levis's *Elegy*, *The Selected Levis*, and *The Gazer Within*" was also a useful source.

Epigraph Sources

Joe Strummer, Mick Jones, Paul Simonon, Topper Headon, "Hate and War," *The Clash* (Epic: 1980).

Alice Fulton, "The Permeable Past Tense Of Feel," *Cascade Experiment: Selected Poems* (W.W. Norton: 2004).

W.H. Auden, "Address to the Beasts," *Collected Poems* (The Modern Library: 1976).

Muriel Rukeyser, "Welcome from War," *The Collected Poems of Muriel Rukeyser* (McGraw-Hill: 1973).

PJ Harvey, "The Glorious Land," *Let England Shake* (Vagrant Records: 2011).

Siegfried Sassoon, "Absolution," *Collected Poems 1908-1956* (Faber & Faber: 1986).

Victor Krummenacher, Greg Lisher, David Lowery, Chris Pedersen, "Sweethearts," *Key Lime Pie* (Virgin Records: 1989).

Acknowledgments

Grateful acknowledgment is made to the editors of the journals in which the following poems previously appeared or are forthcoming:

The Antioch Review: Last Dinner at Louie's with Levis
Bellingham Review: Elegy with Trench Art and Asanas
Beltway Poetry Quarterly: Affinity with Orwell
Birmingham Poetry Review: Resurrection Spell
Blackbird: Angel of Becoming; Landscape and Departure
Bluestem Magazine: Special Screening
The Common: Salt
Connotation Press: An Online Artifact: In Which She Considers
    Joining the Force; Elegy with Civil War Shadowbox
Crazyhorse: Malediction; Portuguese Man o' War
The Earth Project: Et in Arcadia Ego
Green Mountains Review: Object Lessons
Inscape: Triptych (in slightly different form)
Memorious: Souvenir
North Dakota Quarterly: An Ideal for Living; In a Time of Troubles
One: Field Manual for the Forgotten
Per Contra: Parachute Wedding Dress
Poemeleon: A Journal of Poetry: Cursing for Beginners
Southword Journal (Ireland): Radio Clash
String Poet: For Virginia Woolf, March 28, 2011
Unsplendid: Second Angel; Angel of Absence
Verse Wisconsin: Why I Don't Write Nature Poems

"Elegy with Trench Arts and Asanas" was awarded the 49th Parallel Prize from *Bellingham Review*, judged by Kevin Clark.

"Radio Clash" was awarded third prize in the Munster Literature Centre's 2015 Gregory O'Donoghue International Poetry Competition, judged by Matthew Sweeney. The poem was reprinted in *Clash By Night: A London Calling Anthology* (City Lit, 2015).

"Malediction" was a runner-up for the 2015 Lynda Hull Memorial Poetry Prize, judged by Alberto Ríos.

I want to extend thanks to the Virginia Center for the Creative Arts, the Vermont Studio Center, the West Chester University Poetry Conference, Writing the Rockies, the Hyla Brook Poets, and Poetry by the Sea: A Global Conference for welcome support.

For encouragement or suggestions, I extend warm thanks to Kim Bridgford, Dana Curtis, Beth Ann Fennelly, Linda Gregerson, Rachel Hadas, John Hennessy, Adrianne Kalfopoulou, Beth Kephart, Valerie Miner, Dinty Moore, V. Penelope Pelizzon, Kevin Prufer, Jo Shapcott, Adam Vines, Lesley Wheeler, and David Yezzi.

Gracious thanks to Tanja Softić for her generosity in use of *Migrant Universe* as cover art and for her assistance in arranging permissions.

For special kindness during the writing of these poems, thanks to Dan Albergotti, Susan Cohen, Caitlin Doyle, Jehanne Dubrow, Emily Hipchen, Gerry LaFemina, Gary Leising, April Lindner, Debra Marquart, John Nieves, Angela Alaimo O'Donnell, Andrea O'Reilly, Leslie Pietrzyk, Lia Purpura, Kathryn Rhett, David Rothman, David Sanders, Gregg Wilhelm, and Laura Madeline Wiseman.

I'm grateful to longtime colleagues Jean Cole, Kathy Forni, Catriona Hanley, Barbara Mallonee, Nick Miller, Matt Mulcahy, Brian Murray, and Mark Osteen for invaluable support.

Thanks as always to my parents, John and Ellen, and to my siblings and their spouses—Sean and Stasia, Paul and Kama, Pete and Heather, Matt and Lindsey—who lent a helping hand or shared some of the history here. And thanks to Cat for inspiration and for salvaging stray Post-It notes.

Thanks to everyone at Autumn House for editorial guidance. I'm deeply grateful to the amazing David St. John for selecting this book.

Finally, my gratitude to Ned Balbo for his love, encouragement, and editorial eye.

Previous Winners of the Autumn House Poetry Prize

The White Calf Kicks (2003, selected by Naomi Shihab Nye)   **Deborah Slicer**

Dear Good Naked Morning (2004, selected by Alicia Ostriker)   **Ruth L. Schwartz**

lucky wreck (2005, selected by Jean Valentine)   **Ada Limón**

No Sweeter Fat (2006, selected by Tim Seibles)   **Nancy Pagh**

The Dark Opens (2007, selected by Mark Doty)   **Miriam Levine**

A Theory of Everything (2008, selected by Naomi Shihab Nye)   **Mary Crockett Hill**

The Gift That Arrives Broken (2009, selected by Alicia Ostriker)   **Jacqueline Berger**

To Make It Right (2010, selected by Claudia Emerson)   **Corrinne Clegg Hales**

Natural Causes (2011, selected by Denise Duhamel)   **Brian Brodeur**

A Raft of Grief (2012, selected by Stephen Dunn)   **Chelsea Rathburn**

The Moons of August (2013, selected by Naomi Shihab Nye)   **Danusha Laméris**

Practicing the Truth (2014, selected by Alicia Ostriker)   **Ellery Akers**

St. Francis and the Flies (2015, selected by Dorianne Laux)   **Brian Swann**

Apocalypse Mix (2016, selected by David St. John)   **Jane Satterfield**